BOSS DEMYSTIFIED

FROM COMPLEXITY TO CLARITY: MASTER THE ART OF BOSS RELATIONSHIP

ALAP SUDHIR MANKODI

This book is dedicated to my grandparents, parents, my aunt, my wife, and our daughters. Their unwavering support has been my greatest strength and inspiration, and without them, this book would not have been possible.

Contents

Foreword 1

At any stage of one's career, it is impossible to overstate the crucial role that bosses and managers play, not only in determining your quality of life but shaping your career trajectory. According to a study by The Workforce Institute at UKG, which included 3,400 people across 10 countries, 69% of people said their managers had the greatest impact on their mental health. The study revealed that your manager impacts your mental health as much as your life partner does. Given that we spend a large portion of our waking hours at work, it's easy to see why a positive relationship with your immediate superiors is so important.

A 10-year study conducted by the University of Johannesburg revealed that workers with bosses who are inconsiderate, uncommunicative and secretive are 60% more likely to have a heart attack than those with better managers. On the flip side, talented managers can boost productivity by as much as 22%.

Speaking for myself, throughout my career, I have been fortunate enough to have worked with some wonderful bosses who not only offered much-needed guidance and direction but also encouraged me never to give up despite seemingly insurmountable challenges.

As an employee, managing upward and building a solid relationship with your boss is equally important to meet your career aspirations. Of course, bosses are human too, which means they come with their own set of strengths, weaknesses, motivations, and biases. Understanding your boss' personality can equip you better to build a mutually beneficial relationship.

Alap's book on demystifying bosses offers some interesting perspectives and practical tips to help nurture this critical relationship in the life of a professional. As the author has rightly pointed out up front, this book is not about manipulating the boss to gain undue benefits. Rather, it is a guide to fostering a mutual understanding, which will help achieve the company's objectives and goals more efficiently.

I would certainly recommend this book, especially for junior executives who have just started their professional journeys and are learning to navigate the often treacherous and confusing corporate world.

Alap's effortless and conversational style makes this an easy and quick read, with some interesting tidbits for the readers to take away.

Mrs. Arundhati Bhattacharya
Chairperson and CEO of Salesforce India
Former Chairman of the State Bank of India

Foreword 2

Goal of every company is to make more and more money. The role of a team member is to help the team win. - "Leadership is not about titles or positions. It is about inspiring others to get the best out of them. Break paradigm achieve greater heights, fostering a culture of collaboration and innovation, and navigating challenges.

In today's rapidly changing world, there are internal and external challenges. Effective leadership is crucial to success. This book offers valuable insights and practical guidance on understanding various leadership styles and how to handle each effectively.

Alap has very well shared analysis and real-world examples, you'll discover how to:

- Build trust, empathy, and strong relationships.

- Drive positive environment and meet the company goal, through innovation, creativity, and calculated risk-taking

- Navigate uncertainty, ambiguity, and conflict

- Foster a culture of continuous learning and growth

Whether you're an aspiring leader or a seasoned executive, this book will help you equip your skills, confidence, and inspiration to make a lasting impact.

So, embark on this transformative journey, and unlock your full leadership potential and help the team win by achieving its goal.

Mr.Manish Thakur
Former GM
Hyva India Private Limited

Preface

**"People don't leave jobs, they leave bosses."-
Anonymous**

The purpose of this book is not to manipulate the boss-subordinate relationship but to foster mutual understanding, which will help achieve the company's objectives and goals more efficiently. In this context, "boss" refers to the person managing the team (Manager), not to be confused with leadership terms like "leader" or "boss."

Managers, like their subordinates, are affected by various social factors as they navigate their roles within an organization. It is important to recognize that they bear greater responsibilities compared to their subordinates. While it may be challenging to completely avoid the influence of these factors on their daily decisions and behaviours, it is possible to minimize their impact through conscious efforts. This book aims to benefit not only subordinates but also current and future Managers by offering opportunities for introspection and personal growth. By enhancing their behaviors, managers can improve their relationships with their team members, thereby fostering a more positive and productive work environment. This book can be especially helpful in the following ways:

1. **For Existing Managers**: Current managers or leaders can use this book to reflect on their own behaviors and management styles. By identifying areas for improvement and making necessary adjustments, they can boost their team's productivity and efficiency. The book offers practical insights that can help managers become more effective and supportive, ultimately leading to a more engaged and high-performing team.

2. **For Future Managers**: Aspiring managers can benefit from this book by relating its content to their own experiences or observations of different management styles. By understanding the various characteristics and approaches discussed, they can make informed decisions about which practices to adopt and which to avoid, better preparing themselves for effective leadership roles.

3. **For HR Teams**: Human Resources departments often conduct surveys to gather feedback on management performance and team dynamics. This book can provide valuable context for interpreting this feedback by aligning survey results with the types of management styles described. HR teams can use these insights to develop targeted interventions and training programs to improve managerial effectiveness and strengthen team cohesion.

Importance of having a positive Boss – Subordinate relationship:

Maintaining a positive relationship with your boss is crucial, as it can affect both your professional and personal life. Today, employees often spend as much time, if not more, at work than with their families. Here are some key points illustrating the importance of fostering a positive relationship with your boss and how it contributes to a better personal life:

1. **Reduced Stress and Anxiety**
   A good relationship with your boss can help alleviate workplace stress and anxiety. Feeling valued and supported by your superior can reduce work-related pressures, leading to a more relaxed and content state omind. This stress reduction can positively impact your overall mental health, making you happier and more at ease in your personal life.

2. **Enhanced Job Satisfaction**
   Employees with a positive relationship with their boss tend to be more satisfied with their jobs. Job satisfaction is closely linked to life satisfaction. Enjoying your work environment and feeling appreciated can translate into a positive attitude that enhances your personal interactions and relationships outside of work.

3. **Better Work-Life Balance**
   A supportive boss is more likely to recognize the importance of work-life balance and may offer

flexibility with work hours and responsibilities. This flexibility allows you to spend more quality time with family and friends, pursue hobbies, and attend to personal errands, contributing to a more balanced and fulfilling life.

4. **Increased Productivity and Efficiency**
   A good rapport with your boss can lead to improved communication and collaboration, which enhances your productivity and efficiency at work. Being more efficient and productive reduces the need to work late or take work home, giving you more time to relax and enjoy your personal life.

5. **Career Growth and Opportunities**
   A positive relationship with your boss can open doors to career advancement and development opportunities. When a boss mentors and supports your growth, it enhances the likelihood of your professional development, which in turn benefits the organization as a whole.

The names given to different types of bosses are based on the leadership styles and characteristics they exhibit. These traits can range from beneficial to less desirable. In reality, it is common to encounter bosses who display a combination of these traits and personalities. Understanding which behaviours correspond to specific leadership styles helps in recognizing and analysing their effects.

By Identifying these behaviours, it becomes easier to fine-tune one's approach and align strategies to effectively manage and interact with such leaders. This understanding enables individuals to adapt their responses and plan their future actions more strategically, ensuring better alignment with their boss's leadership style and improving overall workplace dynamics.

Acknowledgements

I am deeply grateful to all the mentors and leaders I have had the privilege of working with, each of whom has influenced my understanding of people management. I extend my gratitude to my colleagues and friends, whose insights into their own professional journeys have enriched my perspective.

My special thanks to Mrs. Arundhati Bhattacharya, Chairperson and CEO of Salesforce India and former Chairman of the State Bank of India, and Mr. Manish Thakur, Former GM Hyva India Private Limited, for their thoughtful forewords. I am also thankful to Mr. Sharad Mathur, MD & CEO of Universal Sompo General Insurance Co. Ltd., and Mr. S.S. Rao, CEO of Gujarat University Startup and Entrepreneurship Council, for their valuable suggestions and insights.

The "Methodical Manager" Boss

"A methodical boss sees data not just as numbers, but as the key to unlocking potential and performance." — Anonymous

A methodical manager, also known as a system and process-oriented boss, has distinct characteristics that focus on structure, efficiency, and consistency. Here are some key attributes:

1. **Detail-Oriented**
   Methodical manager pays close attention to details. He ensures every task or project is thoroughly planned and executed. He often uses comprehensive checklists and standard procedures to maintain high standards and reduce errors.

2. **Consistency and Predictability**
   He values consistency and also establishes clear processes and guidelines that are

followed strictly. This predictability helps employees understand what is expected of them and how to achieve their goals.

3. **Strong Organizational Skills**
Methodical Manager is highly organized. He uses tools like project management software, spreadsheets, and calendars to track progress, deadlines, and responsibilities. His organizational skills improves efficiency and streamline operations.

4. **Data-Driven Decision Making**
He relies on data and metrics to make decisions. By analysing performance data and key performance indicators (KPIs), he identifies areas for improvement and implement strategies based on evidence.

5. **Clear Communication**
Methodical manager excels in clear communication. He provides detailed instructions and expectations, ensuring that his team members understand their roles and tasks. Regular updates and feedback keep everyone aligned.

6. **Process Improvement**
He continuously seeks ways to improve processes and systems. This includes identifying inefficiencies, implementing best practices, and staying updated with industry trends and technologies.

7. **Risk Management**
Risk management is crucial for him. He anticipates potential issues and developes contingency plans to manage risks. This

proactive approach helps prevent problems and ensures smoother project execution.

8. **Reliability and Accountability**
Methodical Manager is reliable and holds himself and his teams accountable. He takes ownership of tasks and ensures that everyone is responsible for their contributions to the overall goals.

9. **Emphasis on Training and Development**
Methodical Manager invests in training and development to enhance his team's skills and knowledge. He believes a well-trained team is essential for maintaining high standards and achieving consistent results.

10. **Patience and Persistence**
He is patient and persistent. He understands that building and refining processes take time and is committed to completing projects, even when facing challenges.

Approach as a Team Member

A boss who can transform potential into performance is a tremendous asset, especially at the start of your career. Initially, you might perceive their guidance as excessive or feel that they are "spoon-feeding" you. However, as you advance in your career, you'll come to appreciate the profound impact of his mentorship. The detailed attention and rigorous standards he enforced may have seemed burdensome at the time, but they were crucial for your professional development.

As a team member, your role is to learn and effectively implement the systems and processes that your boss has established. By making an effort to understand the logic and rationale behind these processes, you will find it easier to adapt and follow them without hesitation. When you comprehend the underlying purpose, you're more likely to engage with the system proactively rather than simply going through the motions. In many cases, these systems are designed to produce reliable and even remarkable outcomes, often exceeding expectations, even if they are followed without question. However, understanding the logic behind them can enhance your ability to execute them more effectively and spot areas for improvement.

As you gain more experience and eventually step into a leadership role yourself, you'll recognize the value of the thoroughness and attention to detail that your previous boss demanded. You will likely adopt similar practices, understanding firsthand how such meticulousness contributes to effective team management and overall success. This cycle of learning and applying detailed work is essential for fostering a high-performance team and achieving long-term career growth.

CHAPTER TWO

THE "FRIENDLY FRIEND" BOSS

"A boss who is friendly creates a culture of trust and collaboration, where employees feel motivated and supported." — Anonymous

The "Friendly Friend" Boss is a managerial style characterized by a warm, approachable, and supportive demeanour. Here are some key characteristics:

1. **Approachability and Openness**
   The Friendly Friend Boss maintains an open-door policy, encouraging employees to share their thoughts, concerns, and ideas freely. He creates an environment where team members feel comfortable approaching him without fear of judgment or reprimand.

2. **Empathy and Understanding**
   He demonstrates a high level of empathy and understanding toward his employees. He is attentive to both the personal and professional

needs of his team, showing genuine concern for their well-being and offering support when needed.

3. **Strong Interpersonal Skills**
Friendly Friend Boss excels at building strong, personal relationships with his team members. He takes the time to understand his employees' strengths, weaknesses, and motivations, which helps in fostering a more cohesive and motivated team.

4. **Positive Reinforcement**
The Friendly Friend Boss frequently uses positive reinforcement to acknowledge and appreciate his team's efforts and achievements. He recognizes the power of praise and encouragement in boosting morale and productivity.

5. **Flexibility and Adaptability**
He is flexible and adaptable, willing to adjust his management style to meet the individual needs of his employees. He understands that different situations and personalities require different approaches and is open to accommodating these differences to create a harmonious work environment.

6. **Team-Oriented**
This manager focuses on building a strong sense of team spirit and collaboration. He encourages teamwork and often organizes team-building activities to strengthen bonds among team members, believing in the power of collaboration to achieve goals.

7. **Good Listener**

   The Friendly Friend Boss is an excellent listener. He gives his full attention when employees speak and provide thoughtful and considerate feedback. This active listening helps build trust and respect within the team.

8. **Conflict Resolution**

   He is skilled in conflict resolution, approaching disputes with a calm and rational mindset. He works to understand all perspectives and seek amicable solutions that satisfy everyone, maintaining a peaceful work environment.

9. **Encourages Work-Life Balance**

   He recognizes the importance of work-life balance and encourage his employees to maintain it. He supports flexible working hours and remote work options, understanding that a balanced life leads to happier and more productive employees.

10. **Leads by Example**

    The Friendly Friend Boss leads by example, demonstrating the behaviors and attitudes he wishes to see in his team. He is consistent in his actions and words, fostering an environment of trust and integrity.

Approach as a Team Member

You are truly fortunate if you have a boss who is committed to transforming potential into performance. In such a situation, dedicating yourself fully to your work can yield significant rewards. When your boss observes your commitment and effort, he is likely to support you and advocate on your behalf with higher-ups. His endorsement can open doors and create opportunities for your advancement. When you realize you've made a mistake, it's important to admit it candidly to your boss. "Friendly Friend Boss" will appreciate your honesty and have the strength to address the issue effectively. However, attempting to hide or cover up the mistake can seriously damage trust, which can be incredibly difficult, if not impossible, to fully rebuild.

However, it's important to recognize that this support is contingent upon the overall dynamics within the organization. If the relationship between your boss and his superior deteriorates, it could potentially affect your position and prospects. In such cases, even a strong advocate may find it challenging to shield you from the fallout. Maintaining excellent performance and adapting to changing circumstances will help you navigate these complexities and continue to progress in your career, regardless of external factors.

CHAPTER THREE

THE "MAVERICK MENTOR" BOSS

"A maverick mentor doesn't just lead; they inspire others to question the status quo and create their own path." — Anonymous

The "Maverick Mentor" boss is known for his unique leadership style, blending innovative thinking with a strong commitment to developing his team's skills and potential. Here are some defining characteristics:

1. **Innovative and Forward-Thinking**
   Maverick Mentor is recognized for his creativity and willingness to challenge the status quo. He encourages his team to think outside the box and embrace unconventional solutions. His forward-thinking mindset drives innovation and keeps the team ahead of the curve.
2. **Strong Focus on Mentorship**
   He prioritizes the growth and development of

his team members. He takes a personal interest in mentoring employees, providing guidance, feedback, and opportunities for learning and advancement. His goal is to help each team member reach their full potential.

3. **Encourages Risk-Taking**

   Maverick Mentor fosters an environment where calculated risks are encouraged and failure is viewed as a learning opportunity. He supports his team in experimenting with new ideas and approaches, understanding that innovation often arises from trial and error.

4. **Adaptable and Flexible**

   He is highly adaptable and flexible, able to pivot quickly in response to changing circumstances. This flexibility helps him navigate challenges effectively and seize new opportunities as they arise. His adaptability also extends to his management style, which he tailors to meet the needs of different team members.

5. **Charismatic and Inspirational**

   Maverick Mentor often possesses a charismatic and inspirational presence. He leads by example, inspiring his team with their passion, enthusiasm, and commitment to excellence. His energy and vision motivate employees to strive for their best.

6. **High Emotional Intelligence**

   He has a high degree of emotional intelligence, which enables him to connect with his team on a personal level. He is empathetic, understanding, and skilled at managing interpersonal relationships, creating a supportive and trusting work environment.

7. **Empowering Leadership Style**

   Maverick Mentor empowers his team members by granting them autonomy and responsibility. He trusts his employees to make decisions and take ownership of their work, which boosts confidence and fosters accountability.

8. **Focus on Long-Term Goals**

   Maverick Mentor has a strategic vision and focuses on long-term goals. He helps his team understand how their current tasks and projects fit into the bigger picture, aligning daily activities with the organization's overarching objectives.

9. **Commitment to Continuous Improvement**

   He is committed to continuous improvement, both for themself and his team. He encourages a culture of learning, where team members are constantly seeking to enhance their skills and knowledge. This commitment helps the team stay competitive and effective.

10. **Strong Problem-Solving Skills**

    Maverick Mentor excels at problem-solving. His approaches challenges with a creative and analytical mindset, often coming up with innovative solutions. T His problem-solving skills help his team overcome obstacles and achieve their goals efficiently.

Approach as a Team Member

If your boss is a Maverick Mentor, you have the unique opportunity to fully unleash your creativity. This type of boss encourages innovative thinking and is supportive and understanding, so you can pursue bold ideas without the fear of failure. Knowing that your mentor will guide you and help you learn from any mistakes can be incredibly liberating.

As a team member, it is important to seize every opportunity to take initiative. Your Maverick Mentor will appreciate your proactive approach and willingness to explore new possibilities. By actively participating and contributing ideas, you not only benefit from his support but also play a key role in driving innovation and progress within the team. Embrace the freedom to experiment and take risks, and make the most of the environment he creates, which is designed to foster growth and creativity.

CHAPTER FOUR

THE "UNPREDICTABLE UMBRELLA BOSS"

"Working for an unpredictable boss is a test of adaptability, where stability is found in being flexible and responsive." — Anonymous

The "Unpredictable Umbrella Boss" is known for his erratic and inconsistent management style, which can present both challenges and opportunities for the team. Here are some defining characteristics of this type of boss:

1. **Inconsistent Behaviour**
   Unpredictable Umbrella Boss is recognized for his erratic behaviour. His moods and decisions can shift frequently without warning, making it difficult for employees to anticipate his reactions or understand his expectations.

2. **Impulsive Decision-Making**
   He often makes decisions impulsively and on the spur of the moment. This can result in rapid changes in priorities and directions,

causing confusion and requiring the team to constantly adapt to new plans and strategies.

3. **Lack of Clear Communication**
Clear and consistent communication is frequently lacking with Unpredictable Umbrella Boss. His instructions may be vague or contradictory, leaving employees uncertain about their tasks and responsibilities. This can lead to misunderstandings and mistakes.

4. **High Energy and Creativity**
Despite his unpredictability, he often brings a high level of energy and creativity to his work. His spontaneous ideas and willingness to take risks can lead to innovative solutions and breakthroughs, inspiring his team to think outside the box.

5. **Emotional Volatility**
His emotional state can fluctuate significantly, sometimes resulting in outbursts or erratic displays of emotion. This volatility can create a tense and uncertain work environment, as employees may be unsure how to approach or engage with him on any given day.

6. **Difficulty in Building Trust**
Due to his unpredictable nature, it can be challenging for employees to build a trusting relationship with him. Consistency and reliability are key components of trust, which are often lacking in this management style.

7. **Occasional Micromanagement**
While he may seem disengaged at times, Unpredictable Umbrella Boss can also become intensely involved in the details of his team's

work. This sporadic micromanagement can be stressful and disruptive for employees.

8. **Stressful Work Environment**
   The unpredictability and inconsistency of him can create a high-stress work environment. Employees may feel constantly on edge, unsure of what to expect or how to best meet their boss's expectations.

Approach as a Team Member

Working with an Unpredictable Umbrella Boss can be challenging. Due to his erratic behaviour and inconsistent management style, it is crucial to handle communication carefully. Here are some key strategies to manage this type of boss effectively:

1. **Be Cautious in Communication**
   Given the unpredictability of this type of boss, it's important to be meticulous with communication. Since his behavior can be erratic, you might find that his stance on various issues changes without notice. Always document your interactions and decisions to avoid misunderstandings and to protect yourself if disputes arise in the future.

2. **Request Written Instructions**
   It can be difficult to get clear, written instructions from an Unpredictable Umbrella Boss, but it's highly recommended to do so whenever possible. Written documentation

provides a clear record of what was agreed upon and can help you stay aligned with their expectations. If they are reluctant to provide written instructions, consider summarizing key points from verbal discussions and asking for confirmation in writing.

3. **Confirm Actions in Writing**
   To ensure that your work aligns with his directives, follow up on tasks by communicating in writing what you have done and how it aligns with his instructions. This not only provides a clear record of your efforts but also helps in managing any potential discrepancies or changes in their expectations.

4. **Maintain a Record of Communication**
   Keep a detailed log of your communications, including emails, memos, and any other written exchanges. This record will be valuable if there are disputes or if you need to clarify what was previously discussed.

5. **Stay Flexible and Adaptable**
   Due to the unpredictable nature of this boss, remaining flexible and adaptable is essential. Be prepared to adjust your plans and strategies as needed while maintaining a professional demeanour.

By being proactive and diligent in your communication, you can better navigate the challenges posed by an Unpredictable Umbrella Boss and protect yourself from potential issues that may arise due to his inconsistent management style.

CHAPTER FIVE

The "Verbal Vaporizer" Boss

"A boss whose words are laced with venom spreads distrust and discontent through the team." — Anonymous

The "Verbal Vaporizer" boss is known for his intense and often abrasive communication style. Here are the key characteristics of this type of boss:

1. **Aggressive Communication**
   The Verbal Vaporizer boss frequently uses a harsh and aggressive tone. He may raise his voice, employ strong language, and display a confrontational demeanour, which can be intimidating for employees.

2. **Frequent Criticism**
   This boss is quick to criticize and highlight mistakes in a blunt, direct manner. His feedback often comes across as harsh and demoralizing rather than constructive,

negatively impacting employee morale.

3. **Lack of Emotional Intelligence**

   He typically exhibits low levels of emotional intelligence, struggling to recognize or empathize with his employees' feelings. This lack of empathy can make him seem uncaring and detached from his team's well-being.

4. **Impatience**

   Verbal Vaporizer is often highly impatient, demanding quick results and immediate responses. His impatience can lead to unrealistic expectations and increased pressure on employees to meet tight deadlines.

5. **Dominance and Control**

   This boss tends to dominate conversations and decision-making processes, leaving little room for employee input or collaboration. His needs for control can stifle creativity and innovation within the team.

6. **Unpredictable Outbursts**

   Employees may feel they are walking on eggshells around a Verbal Vaporizer boss due to his unpredictable emotional outbursts. This volatility can create a tense and unstable work environment.

7. **High Standards**

   Although his communication style is abrasive, this boss often sets very high-performance standards. He pushes his employees to achieve excellence, though the pressure can be overwhelming and counterproductive.

8. **Intimidation Tactics**

   Verbal Vaporizer boss may use intimidation

to assert their authority and maintain control. This can involve threats of job loss, public reprimands, or other coercive behaviours.

9. **Poor Listening Skills**
He often exhibits poor listening skills, focusing more on expressing his own opinions and directives than on understanding or considering others' perspectives. This can lead to miscommunication and ineffective teamwork.

10. **High Turnover**
Teams led by Verbal Vaporizer boss frequently experience high turnover rates. The stressful and hostile work environment can drive employees to seek other opportunities, resulting in a continuous cycle of recruitment and training.

Approach as a Team Member

Handling a Verbal Vaporizer boss can be challenging both professionally and emotionally, as he tends to prioritize numbers and results over interpersonal dynamics. The best approach for managing such a boss involves focusing on delivering tangible outcomes and demonstrating your contributions clearly.

Here are some strategies to effectively manage this type of boss:

1. **Showcase Your Work**
   Continuously highlight your accomplishments and progress. Regularly update him on your work to ensure they see the results of your efforts.

2. **Manage Commitments Wisely**
   Avoid over-promising and under-delivering. Instead, set realistic expectations by under-promising and then exceeding those expectations. This approach helps build credibility and reduces the risk of criticism.

3. **Protect Your Well-being**
   Use active listening skills to understand his demands and feedback without letting his harsh communication affect your health. Maintain a professional distance to safeguard your emotional well-being.

4. **Prepare for Diverse Work Environments**
   Working with a Verbal Vaporizer boss can be an intense experience, but it can also equip you with the skills to handle various personalities and management styles. If you can navigate the challenges posed by such a boss, you'll be well-prepared to work effectively with a range of different leaders.

CHAPTER SIX

THE "DECEPTIVE DIRECTOR"

"When a boss backs out, it's not just the promises that are broken; it's the trust." — Anonymous

The "Deceptive Director" or "Paltibaz Boss" is known for a manipulative and often dishonest approach to management. This type of boss uses various tactics to control and influence their team, often prioritizing their interests over those of their employees. Here are some key characteristics:

1. **Manipulative Behaviour**
   The Deceptive Director employs psychological tactics to manipulate and control his employees. He might pit team members against each other, spread misinformation, or use flattery and deceit to achieve their objectives.

2. **Dishonesty**

   This boss is frequently dishonest, bending the truth or outright lying to serve his purposes. He may make promises he has no intention of keeping or provide misleading information to manage perceptions and outcomes.

3. **Inconsistent and Unpredictable**

   This boss is known for his inconsistency and unpredictability. He may frequently change his stance or directives, making it challenging for employees to understand expectations or know where they stand.

4. **Favouritism and Bias**

   Favouritism is common with this boss, who gives preferential treatment to certain employees while neglecting others. This behaviour can create a toxic work environment, leading to resentment and reduced team cohesion and morale.

5. **Gaslighting**

   Gaslighting is a tactic often used by Deceptive Director. He manipulates situations to make employees doubt their perceptions and judgments, thereby maintaining control and undermining the team's confidence.

6. **Lack of Accountability**

   Deceptive Director rarely takes responsibility for his actions. He is quick to blame others for mistakes and failures, deflecting criticism and avoiding accountability. This behaviour can demoralize employees and erode trust within the team.

7. **Opportunistic**

This type of boss is highly opportunistic, always seeking ways to benefit himself at others' expense. He may take credit for others' work, exploit situations to his advantage, and make decisions that serve his own interests rather than those of the team or organization.

8. **Undermining and Sabotage**

This boss may deliberately undermine or sabotage employees he views as threats or those who do not align with his plans. This can include withholding information, providing incorrect instructions, or setting unrealistic expectations to ensure failure.

9. **Lack of Transparency**

Transparency is often lacking with Deceptive Director. He keeps employees in the dark about key decisions, changes, or plans, creating an environment of uncertainty and mistrust.

10. **Erosion of Team Morale**

The manipulative and dishonest tactics of the Deceptive Director can severely damage team morale. Employees may feel undervalued, mistrusted, and demotivated, leading to decreased productivity and high turnover rates.

Approach as a Team Member

This type of boss is detrimental not only to his team members but also to the organizations he represents. His impact extends beyond internal team dynamics to affect client relationships and overall organizational health. Here's a detailed look at the various ways in which his behaviour can be harmful:

1. **Miscommunication and Mismanagement**
   Deceptive Director often lacks clear communication, both with his team and with customers. This can lead to significant miscommunication, where the boss may provide inaccurate or misleading information, causing confusion and errors in project execution.

2. **Financial Repercussions**
   Team members might face financial difficulties due to the boss's inconsistent or dishonest promises. For instance, employees may be instructed to incur expenses on behalf of the company or customers with the assurance that these costs will be reimbursed. However, when it comes time to approve these expenses, the boss may refuse to authorize the reimbursement, leaving employees to bear the financial burden themselves.

3. **Damage to Client Relationships**
   The behaviour of a Deceptive Director can negatively impact client relationships. If a

boss's deceitful or erratic behaviour reflects poorly on the company, clients may associate these issues with the organization as a whole. This can lead to strained client relationships, lost business opportunities, and damage to the company's reputation.

4. **Risk to Major Deals**
   The boss's manipulative tactics and lack of transparency can jeopardize significant deals. Clients may perceive the boss's behaviour as indicative of the company's overall approach, leading to distrust and potential loss of major contracts or business opportunities.

5. **Internal and External Reputation Damage**
   Both the internal morale and external reputation of the organization can suffer due to the Deceptive Director's actions. Internally, team members may become demotivated and frustrated, while externally, clients and partners may lose confidence in the company's reliability and professionalism.

To avoid repercussions such as miscommunication, mismanagement, financial losses, damaged client relations, the risk of losing major deals, and the potential harm to both internal and external reputations, it is essential to have all communications and instructions in writing. A deceptive director boss may avoid giving problematic instructions in writing, so it is best to confirm the execution of his instructions through email or formal communication to ensure there is an official record. Never follow his instructions blindly, as he may deny giving such directives if the desired outcome is not achieved. If you regularly share updates on successes via email, while appreciating your boss's verbal inputs, and copy his reporting manager where appropriate, it helps to foster a culture of open communication. This practice makes it natural and transparent to document any verbal instructions, whether or not you're fully convinced about them. By creating this open communication habit, you're not just protecting yourself from potential future misunderstandings or shifts in responsibility, but also contributing to a collaborative and transparent work environment. This helps build trust and ensures that everyone is aligned, making it easier to address any concerns openly and without apprehension. Dealing with such boss can be challenging, but if you have no choice but to work under him, it's crucial to ensure that all instructions are communicated and documented in writing.

CHAPTER SEVEN

THE "WHIMSY WIZARD" BOSS

"A charismatic boss has the power to light up the room with their presence, transforming ordinary moments into extraordinary experiences." — Anonymous

The "Whimsy Wizard" boss is known for their eccentric, imaginative, and unpredictable leadership style. He brings a unique blend of creativity and spontaneity to his role, often infusing the work environment with a sense of playfulness and magic. Here are some defining characteristics of this type of boss:

1. **Highly Creative**
   Whimsy Wizard boss is exceptionally creative and innovative. He encourages his team to think outside the box and explore unconventional ideas. His imaginative approach often leads to unique solutions and a dynamic work environment.

2. **Playful and Fun-Loving**
Whimsy Wizard infuses the workplace with fun and playfulness. He might organize spontaneous team activities, theme days, or other whimsical events to boost morale and create a joyful work environment.

3. **Inspirational and Motivating**
His enthusiasm and passion are infectious. He inspires and motivates his team by sharing their vision and excitement for projects. His positive energy can significantly boost team morale and foster a strong sense of camaraderie.

4. **Flexible and Adaptable**
This boss is highly adaptable and open to new ideas and changes. He is not bound by rigid rules or procedures, allowing him to pivot quickly in response to new opportunities or challenges.

5. **Visionary Thinking**
Whimsy Wizard boss often has a grand vision for the future. He is forward-thinking and strives to push boundaries, aiming to achieve extraordinary results. His visionary thinking can inspire his team to reach new heights.

6. **Encourages Creativity and Innovation**
He cultivates an environment that fosters creativity and innovation. Employees are given the freedom to experiment and take risks without fear of failure, promoting a culture of continuous improvement and growth.

7. **High Emotional Intelligence**
Whimsy Wizard typically possesses high

emotional intelligence. He is empathetic, understanding, and able to connect with his team on a personal level. This helps build strong relationships and a supportive work culture.

8. **Charismatic Leadership**
This boss has a charismatic and magnetic personality. His charm and wit makes him likable and respected leader. He uses his charisma to inspire and effectively influence his team.

9. **Balancing Work and Play**
He values the importance of balancing work and play. By integrating fun and creativity into the workplace, he keeps his team engaged and motivated, reducing stress and preventing burnout.

Approach as a Team Member

The presence of this type of boss is palpable not only in face-to-face meetings but also in virtual interactions. His strong aura enables him to achieve results from anyone in the organization, even under the most challenging conditions. He offers support to his team members not just in professional matters but also on a personal level. He takes the time to know each team member by name and inquire about the well-being of family members. His commitment to team extends beyond the workplace, as he is willing to go the extra mile to provide support.

This type of boss is highly approachable, even after you have moved on from their team or the organization. He actively leads corporate outdoor training programs and enthusiastically participates in activities designed to motivate the team. He possesses the unique ability to bring out the best in each team member.

If you have the opportunity to work with such a boss, embrace it fully. Leverage his support not only for your professional growth but also for personal and social development. You should feel fortunate to have found a mentor who is invested in your success both inside and outside of work.

CHAPTER EIGHT

THE "GLORY GRABBER" BOSS

"A credit-taking boss may enjoy the accolades, but they sacrifice the respect and loyalty of their team in the process." — Anonymous

The "Glory Grabber" boss is characterized by his tendency to claim credit for the work and achievements of his team members. This type of boss can have a significantly negative impact on team morale and productivity. Here are some key characteristics of a Glory Grabber boss:

1. **Takes Credit for Others' Work**
   Glory Grabber boss often claims credit for his employees' ideas, projects, and successes. He presents himself as the driving force behind the team's achievements, frequently ignoring or downplaying the contributions of others.
2. **Lack of Recognition**
   This boss rarely acknowledges or recognizes

the hard work and efforts of his team members. This lack of recognition can demotivate employees, leading to resentment and frustration within the team.

3. **Self-Promotion**

He is highly focused on self-promotion and personal advancement. Glory Grabber excels at presenting himself in a favourable light to upper management and stakeholders, often leveraging his team's accomplishments to enhance their profile.

4. **Undermines Team Collaboration**

The Glory Grabber's behaviour can undermine trust and collaboration within the team. Employees may be less inclined to share ideas or work together if they believe their contributions will be appropriated by their boss.

5. **Insecure Leadership**

Often, the behaviour of a Glory Grabber boss is driven by insecurity. He may feel threatened by the talent and success of his team members, leading him to take credit for achievements as a way to preserve his position and reputation.

6. **Micromanagement**

Glory Grabber boss may engage in micromanagement to stay closely involved in every aspect of a project. This allows him to position himself as the key figure in any resulting success, further marginalizing his team's contributions.

7. **Poor Team Morale**

The appropriation of credit and lack of

recognition can severely affect team morale. Employees who feel undervalued are likely to become disengaged and less productive over time.

8. **High Turnover Rates**
    Teams led by Glory Grabber boss often experience high turnover rates. Talented employees who feel their work is not recognized or valued are more likely to leave for environments where their contributions are appreciated.

9. **Competitive Environment**
    His behaviour can foster a competitive rather than collaborative environment. Employees may feel compelled to compete for recognition and visibility, leading to unhealthy competition and conflict within the team.

10. **Damage to Team Reputation**
    While a Glory Grabber boss might initially appear successful, his actions can ultimately damage the team's reputation. When the contributions of talented employees are not acknowledged, the overall perception of the team's capabilities and effectiveness can suffer.

Approach as a Team Member

If you have a boss with these characteristics, it's crucial to exercise caution and adopt specific strategies to protect yourself and maintain your well-being. Here's a detailed approach to managing this challenging situation:

1. **Document Everything**
   Be meticulous about documenting your work and the support you require. Keep written records of your achievements, contributions, and any requests for assistance. This documentation serves as evidence in case your boss attempts to take credit for your work or shifts blame onto you for issues beyond your control.

2. **Regular Updates**
   Provide regular written updates on your progress and achievements. This keeps a clear record of your contributions and ensures that your boss cannot easily appropriate your work without acknowledgment. Regular updates also serve as a defensive measure against unfair criticism.

3. **Seek Written Confirmation**
   Whenever you receive instructions or support from your boss, request written confirmation. This helps in clarifying expectations and provides a record of agreed-upon actions or approvals. Written confirmations can also safeguard you if issues arise later.

4. **Maintain Professionalism**
   It's essential to remain calm and composed, even when dealing with your boss's illogical behaviour. Emotional reactions can exacerbate the situation and negatively impact your health and family life. Strive to keep interactions professional and focused on work-related matters.

5. **Manage Stress**
   Recognize the potential impact of working with such a boss on your mental and physical health. Develop coping strategies to manage stress effectively, such as engaging in regular exercise, practicing mindfulness, or seeking support from friends, family, or a counsellor.

6. **Protect Your Well-being**
   Ensure that the stress from your work environment does not negatively affect your personal life. Set boundaries to maintain a healthy work-life balance and engage in activities outside of work that bring you joy and relaxation.

7. **Evaluate Your Options**
   Continuously assess whether the work environment is sustainable for you in the long term. If the negative impact on your well-being becomes overwhelming, consider exploring alternative opportunities where your contributions are valued and recognized.

CHAPTER NINE

The "Egomaniac Executive" Boss

"An egomaniac boss can turn a thriving team into a group of silent followers, stifling innovation and collaboration." — Anonymous

The "Egomaniac Executive" boss is characterized by an inflated sense of self-importance and a constant need for admiration and validation. Here are the defining traits of this type of boss:

1. **Self-Centeredness**
   Egomaniac Executive is highly self-centred, prioritizing his own needs, opinions, and achievements above those of others. He views himself as the central figure in the organization and expects everyone to acknowledge and affirm his superiority.
2. **Need for Constant Praise**
   This boss requires ongoing praise and validation. He actively seeks recognition for

his accomplishments and may react negatively if he feels he is not receiving sufficient admiration from his team and peers.

3. **Micromanagement**

Believing he is the most competent, Egomaniac Executive often engages in micromanagement. He struggles to delegate tasks and insists on overseeing every detail of his team's work, which can stifle creativity and autonomy.

4. **Dismissive of Others' Ideas**

He frequently dismisses others' ideas and contributions, considering his ideas to be superior. This attitude can hinder innovation and collaboration within the team, as employees may feel their input is undervalued.

5. **Intolerance to Criticism**

Egomaniac Executive is highly intolerant of criticism. He may respond defensively or aggressively when his decisions or actions are questioned, which discourages open communication and honest feedback.

6. **Manipulative Behaviour**

He can be manipulative, using his influence and authority to control situations and people to his advantage. This behaviour can create a toxic work environment where employees feel exploited and powerless.

7. **Focus on Personal Achievement**

His primary focus is on his own personal achievements and career advancement. He often prioritizes projects and tasks that enhance his reputation rather than those that benefit the team or organization as a whole.

8. **Lack of Empathy**
   Egomaniac Executive typically lacks empathy. He is more concerned with his feelings and perspectives and often fails to understand or appreciate the emotions and needs of his employees.

9. **Competitive Nature**
   He has a highly competitive nature, always striving to outshine others. This competitiveness can foster unhealthy rivalry within the team and undermine cooperation and team spirit.

10. **High Turnover Rates**
    Teams led by Egomaniac Executive often experience high turnover rates. The lack of recognition, and empathy, and the hostile work environment can drive talented employees to seek employment elsewhere, leading to frequent turnover and a loss of valuable skills and experience.

Approach as a Team Member:

Dealing with an Egomaniac Executive can be challenging, as this boss is highly vulnerable both to his team and to the organization. Here's a detailed approach to handling such boss:

1. **Understand His Ego Triggers**
   To effectively manage your relationship with an Egomaniac Executive, it is crucial to

understand what triggers his ego. By identifying what feeds his need for admiration and validation, you can tailor your interactions to align with his ego, thereby influencing his behaviour more favourably.

2. **Navigate His Ego**

   Once you grasp the nuances of his ego, you can strategically manage your interactions to maintain a positive relationship. This might involve subtly highlighting his contributions or achievements, making him feel valued, and positioning yourself in a way that aligns with his sense of self-importance.

3. **Act as a Pseudo-Boss**

   By addressing his ego effectively, you might find yourself in a position where you are granted significant authority. If you manage his ego well, you could operate almost as a pseudo-boss, enjoying a degree of influence while ensuring that his ego is consistently stroked.

4. **Maintain Vigilance**

   Be cautious and vigilant in your interactions. An Egomaniac Executive can turn hostile if he perceives that his ego is being threatened or ignored. Regularly assess the dynamics of your relationship and adapt your approach to avoid any actions that might trigger his negative reactions.

5. **Impact on Organizational Decisions**

   An excessive focus on ego can sometimes lead leader to make decision that negatively impact the organization. When his primary concern is satisfying his own ego, it can overshadow broader organizational goals, resulting in poor decision-making that harms overall performance. As a team member, it can be challenging, but it's important to tactfully inform him when a decision might not serve the organization's best interests. You can guide him towards reconsidering by framing your feedback in a way that allows him to see how the decision could be improved to align with both his personal pride and the company's objectives. By relating the better outcome to his sense of achievement or success, you can help him adjust his decisions without feeling threatened.

This requires a deep understanding of his ego and how it influences his thinking. You will likely encounter several such situations, so the key is to develop a diplomatic approach that balances honesty with sensitivity. By managing his ego strategically, you can help steer decisions in the right direction while maintaining a productive relationship.

1. **Unawareness of His Ego**
    One of the most challenging aspects of working with an egotistical executive is that they are often unaware of the extent of his own ego. He may not fully recognize how his behavior and decisions impact others or the organization. Building a personal rapport and

finding common areas of interest can create a stronger bond, allowing you to tactfully address the repercussions of decisions driven by ego without directly confronting or hurting his pride. This rapport helps create an environment where you can offer constructive feedback more freely.

If you succeed in influencing a decision and that change results in positive outcomes—especially in a situation where an ego-driven decision may have led to negative consequences—you can use this as an opportunity to subtly highlight the benefits of making choices based on organizational interests rather than personal ego. This gentle reinforcement can help him become more aware of the value of thoughtful decision-making. Over time, this approach can serve as a reference point when you need to guide him away from ego-driven choices, reinforcing the idea that adjusting his decisions can lead to better outcomes for both his success and the organization's success.

CHAPTER TEN

THE "THRIVING-ON-CHAOS" BOSS

"In every crisis, there's an opportunity to innovate and improve." – Anonymous.

A **Thriving-on-Chaos Boss** or A Man on Mission Boss is a leader who excels in unpredictable, fast-paced, and often chaotic environments. Here are some key characteristics and qualities of such a leader:

1. **Adaptability**: Such a boss is brought to the scene when the company is in a mess. Such a boss is capable of deliberately creating a chaotic work environment to realign the team to separate the grain from the chaff. However, they can quickly adjust to changing circumstances and make decisions on the fly, embracing uncertainty rather than fearing it.

2. **Creativity**: In chaotic situations, he often thinks outside the box, coming up with innovative solutions that others might overlook.

3. **High Energy**: He draws motivation and enthusiasm from challenges, often creating an energetic atmosphere that encourages their team to push beyond their boundaries.

4. **Strong Problem-Solving Skills**: He is adept at identifying issues and finding effective solutions, even in high-pressure situations.

5. **Leadership Under Pressure**: This leader remains calm and focused during crises, instilling confidence in his team and guiding them through turbulence.

6. **Empowerment**: He encourages his team members to take initiative and make decisions, fostering a sense of ownership and collaboration.

7. **Visionary Thinking**: He can see opportunities where others see obstacles, often turning chaotic situations into chances for growth and innovation.

8. **Communication Skills**: He communicates clearly and effectively, ensuring that his team understands goals and expectations, even when circumstances are unclear.

9. **Ruthlessness**: He is ruthless in his approach to work. He will not hesitate to fire anyone found with lethargy, sub-optimal output or politics within his team. He is also quick to appreciate and reward performers. Because of this approach, his team has a very high level of

motivation and entrepreneurship.

Approach as a Team Member

Working with a thriving-on-chaos boss requires both courage and a deep understanding of his unique approach to leadership. To truly thrive in this environment, you need to be observant and recognize the subtle yet positive changes occurring within the organization. When you begin to notice improvements in areas such as policy, standard operating procedures (SOPs), and people management, it becomes easier to appreciate and accept this type of leadership.

This boss is proactive, always seeking opportunities for change and improvement. He is present wherever transformation is needed, encouraging a culture of open communication. It takes courage to share concerns about what isn't working in your department or the organization at large, but this boss welcomes constructive feedback. He is receptive to new ideas and appreciate team members who bring solutions to the table.

When expressing your opinions, it's beneficial to frame your input assertively. Instead of saying, "I feel" or "I think," use "I recommend." This communicates confidence and demonstrates that you have thoughtfully considered your perspective.

Working with a thriving-on-chaos boss offers a valuable opportunity for growth. By understanding his actions and the rationale behind decisions, you can align yourself with his vision. If you embrace responsibility and engage with his dynamic approach, you may find yourself not only contributing to the success of the organization but also rising to new heights in your career. With his guidance, you have the potential to build something great together.

CHAPTER ELEVEN

THE "BUREAUCRATIC" BOSS

"Comfort zones are cozy places, but nothing ever grows there."-Anonymous

The description outlines a type of boss characterized by a lack of initiative and rigid adherence to instructions from higher management. This individual possesses knowledge and expertise but tends to follow directives without critically assessing their validity, logic, or appropriateness. Consequently, this boss expects team members to adopt a similarly compliant approach, discouraging any dissent or independent thought.

If team members raise valid concerns or suggest alternative methods that may enhance productivity or effectiveness, this boss may respond defensively, often reporting dissent to his superior. This cycle can create a stifling work environment where innovation is suppressed, and team members feel discouraged from voicing their opinions.

Such leadership behaviours are frequently observed in public sector or government organizations, where job security is less dependent on performance metrics. In these settings, the absence of competitive pressures can lead to a culture that favours conformity over initiative, often resulting in inefficiencies and disengagement among team members. A lack of accountability for poor performance may further entrench these behaviours, as there is often little incentive for leaders to adapt, innovate, or improve their managerial style.

Approach as a Team Member

If you are brimming with energy, creativity, and a strong drive for career advancement, working under a bureaucratic or puppet boss may not be the best use of your talents. If you hold on to the hope that this boss will eventually retire or transfer (which often doesn't happen), consider whether it's worth the wait. Remaining in such an environment can stifle your potential and ultimately hinder your career growth.

On the other hand, if you find comfort in complacency and enjoy staying within your comfort zone, this type of boss might suit you well. In that case, simply agreeing with everything—essentially saying "Yes, Boss"—can make you a favored team member. You might even appear to thrive in his eyes, as you meet his expectations for compliance and adherence to established protocols.

For those who wish to navigate this dynamic more strategically, adopting a diplomatic approach can be effective. If you can demonstrate to your boss that your decisions will not jeopardize his position as the "blue-eyed boy" in the eyes of higher management, you may find that he will allow you greater autonomy. By ensuring he feels secure and appreciated, you can work more freely while minimizing his interference in your projects.

Conclusion:

No single truth defines a person; each individual embodies multiple facets of reality. The same applies to all the different types of bosses mentioned in this book. A boss may exhibit a mix of characteristics, with one being primary and another secondary. Over time, as both the boss and the team members work together, they may adapt their styles. Thus, any perceived changes in the boss's behaviour might reflect the boss's growth and the team member's adjustments.

At times, a boss may introspect and recognize areas for improvement, leading to noticeable shifts in his behaviour. Various factors—such as age, health, family dynamics, and other social influences—can contribute to these changes. Being a boss is a continuously evolving journey, much like parenting. No book can make you a perfect boss, but it can serve as a mirror, offering you a chance to reflect and grow.

As a current or future boss, you might be tempted to replicate the traits you experienced as a team member. However, rather than simply imitating others, you should strive to cultivate your own leadership style, drawing lessons from the bosses you've worked with. Ultimately, leadership is about achieving the organization's goals, with everyone collaborating as a team. By reading this book and reflecting on your leadership approach, we can create a culture within the organization where every day feels like 'Boss Day,' celebrating progress, leadership, and teamwork.

www.ingramcontent.com/pod-product-compliance
Lightning Source LLC
Chambersburg PA
CBHW031507150726
47990CB00007B/2904